Take Control of your Tomorrow

Other books by Dr Funke Baffour

Good Monday Morning

Love your Authentic Self -A 10 Step Guide

Improving your Thinking -A 10 Step Guide

Take Control of your Tomorrow

Dr Funke Baffour

Published by: dftakecontrol

First edition: 2011

Second edition 2016

ISBN: 9780956977151

Acknowledgments

First and foremost I would like to thank my creator for enabling me to tap into a resource I never knew existed. Each day I learn how empowering this resource is.

I like to thank all my family members, particularly my wonderful husband, Kwaku, our son, Osei and daughter, Amankwah; my siblings Bola, Lanre and Gbenga.

I would also like to thank the following people for their supportive editorial comments, Natika Halil, Rita Wright, Wonu Sanda, Bonnie Samuels, Anne-Marie-Reid Kofi, Gillian Lonsdale, Jodie Ellis, Jennifer Willbaforce, Ann Beavis, Alicia Johnson and Matilda Koroma.

Dedications

On completion of the first draft of this book in 2009, I had dedicated it to my late father and my young brother Ade-Wusi. However, the latter part of 2009 my mother died unexpectedly; followed by my older brother six months later who died unexpectedly. All the losses in my life have indeed had a great impact on me; however I am very thankful that I have been able to turn my grief into something that I can share with others in order to help them. One thing that I do know is that there are some things in life that we have no control over, however I do believe that we can eventually take control of the way we deal with such things in life.

A final dedication is to all of you for embarking on this journey to Take Control of your Tomorrow!

Contents

Foreword

As I read through the final draft of this book I found myself reflecting on my own life all over again. I realised the more questions I posed, the more clarity I found in the answers. These new illuminating insights helped me to make some significant and life-changing decisions that led me to recognise that no matter how bleak things seemed, I had the ability to change the outcome. To know I had more control regarding my perceptions of my life was very liberating.

Life, I realised, was as much about perception and attitude as anything else. If I could change a negative, however bad, into a positive, I knew this meant I was moving towards the light. It was a revelation. It was as if a light-bulb had pinged on in my head. Just as day follows night, this chain of events took me from an anxious place to somewhere calm, and the ripple effect is leading me to a happier and healthier lifestyle. I am still on a journey and I haven't arrived yet but that is OK. I guess that sometimes it's OK to not be OK.

One of my first books, 'Good Monday Morning', was written as an inspirational fix to what is often looked upon as a bleak day of the week. I enjoyed this process but knew I wanted to write more — to go deeper — to add another dimension that could really help others to change their lives. I thought about us human beings and our thought process, and how we have evolved into very different creatures with additional needs and desires to those of our fore-fathers.

Why are so many of us consumed with anxiety and depression? Why do we feel such little satisfaction? Why do so many people feel out of control and resort to acting out emotions and feelings? So many questions — the answers to which I hope you will find in this book. A book which aims to ease you into the driving seat of your life, and help you steer yourself to a 'good enough' understanding of what is personally going on in your world; as well as how you fit into the world around you. I don't advocate this book will answer all your questions but what it will do is help you acquire the tools of the trade to help you deal with LIFE!

Writing this book has been empowering — a true revelation for me. My hope is that your experience will mirror mine. I hope you reflect as much as I did about the many aspects of my life, and like me, ask yourself, "What changes do I need to make to enable myself to push forward in this tricky world and find peace and harmony?"

We are always finding new ways to lead more healthy lives. Sometimes this concerns our physical health, other times our mental well-being; often the physiology and psychology are entwined as we attempt to refine who we are. I guess, ultimately, this book is about being truthful to ourselves. About learning to recognise when we need to take time out and consider what is right for us at that particular moment.

When I feel the desire to go back to basics, I consciously take myself back to my authentic self – the real me – the person I was before painful life experiences made their mark. I can't impress on you enough the importance of this exercise. It keeps you grounded and in touch with a part of yourself you must not lose. If you sense you have already lost it, let me reassure you – your authentic self might get buried for a while but it never truly deserts you. It is always lurking somewhere beneath the troubles.

So what is it that is keeping you stuck in a 'self' that you are uncomfortable with? There you are, going from day to day, chasing round and round the hamster's wheel, until you reach the point of exhaustion! Try another image. See yourself sitting in a rocking chair with that old thief of time and procrastination for company. What is keeping you confined to the chair? Is it a case that you are holding on to past hurt, or trying to control external situations?

Now, visualise yourself taking charge of the essential things in your life and really 'going for it'. I have a feeling this will become the driving force that propels you towards your God given destiny – health and happiness.

In my lifetime I have been blessed in so many ways, and I am eternally grateful that I possess a deep faith in God and all He stands for. Throughout this book, as in my life, I highlight how my Creator has accompanied me through a wilderness where, once upon a time, my eyes did not want to open and I felt as if I was gasping for my last breath. During these lost times, when life seemed unfair and unjust, I kept on going...and going...and people would ask me in astonishment, "Funke, where on earth do get your energy from?" After pondering on these observations, the only plausible answer I could come up with as to how I managed to come out the other end of grief and sadness with my sanity intact was my love of life and a deep yearning for even more guidance from my Creator. This may seem too simplistic, but then the most important things in life are simple – it just takes a while to know it!

Every breath we take is a representation that we are living human beings. What and who we are depends on our own perception of ourselves – not that of others. We thus have the ability to change what we do not like and what is not working for us.

There are times when I am faced with challenges where I not only have to question my motives, but also take the time to be silent and sit with the uncomfortable feelings that I instinctively want to run from. I tell myself I am stronger than I think and that I don't need to resort to short cuts that will give me short term instant gratification, but seek a long-lasting sense of satisfaction.

I sincerely hope that reading this book will give you a similar sense of satisfaction that I gained from the process of writing it – and that you find your very own light-bulb moments where it's not the switching on, but the turning of the pages that lights your space.

Ready Steady Go...

One of the philosophies I hold dear is that you can't actually teach anyone anything; you can only help them find their own wisdom. If you, the reader, can become a confident 'learner', then I can teach you the skills you need to carry on learning. So let's explore, and let's enjoy as we go along.

How much of what you think you are is based on your own interpretation?

This might sound crazy. You might ask yourself, "How can I be anything other than what I really think I am?" Yet, from the moment we are born we are programmed to be what others want or believe us to be.

Here's another question. "What do you imagine was written above your crib when you were born? Were you destined to be the child who lived out his father's unfulfilled dreams? Or were you going to be the kid who was going down the same road to self-destruction like some members of your family.

Think about it. Let this be your first reflection in this book. Imagine you are in the rocking chair by the window looking out to the light. Feel what comes through to you. Just like me, you may be stronger than you think. Keep on believing.

As you embark on this journey of discovery, imagine all the other people in the world seeking a happier and truer sense of self, doing the same thing – getting in touch with their authentic self. Know that you are not alone. You may feel lost and lonely but you are not alone. We all hurt. Life is tough. Remember: It is not what life throws at you, as much as how you perceive it and deal with it.

A word of warning!

Many people are fearful of change. When you embark on this journey and you begin to change, some people may well be thrown off kilter. Your motives are likely to be questioned, and how you conduct yourself, if different to before, might be challenged. Keep in mind the old saying – fore-warned is fore-armed, and don't give up.

This is you finally letting them know you have decided who you want to be rather than what they need you to be. Their sense of loss will be your gain. Soon you will be ready to shake off the mind-traps that have bound and gagged you for so long. The thing to remember is that your growth may well facilitate theirs. How wonderful is that?

One of the most intriguing things I've found in both my professional and personal life is the lack of motivation people have in their lives. Too often they begin something, only to abandon it soon afterwards. Others hold on for longer, but then they too fall short of reaching their goals. This can be self-defeating and of course tiresome.

My friends refer to me as a 'go-getter'. Others ask, "Where do you get this zest for life from?" They don't realise that I too, from time to time, fall into the same trap – that it is an ongoing issue for each and every one of us that we have to work hard at conquering.

Satisfaction in this book derives from a fundamental ethos that life is a precious gift and each day I want this gift to blossom. It is as simple as that, and it is my desire to pass on and to share this zing for life.

Bookshops are piled high with self-help books. We can't get enough of them. We live in an era where day to day stress leads to mental health problems; and in an effort to survive we naturally keep on seeking answers. In this book, I am offering more than a recapitulation of other motivational books. My focus is on helping you to release the power that lies inside your authentic self.

So, each page of this book offers bite-sized inspirational summaries to help you to access the real you. My hope is that it gives you the light you need to kick start and enjoy opportunities that will occur once you adopt the philosophy that each day can lead to finding the real you.

Enjoy this journey of self-discovery!

Learn to let it go

Will power does not give you the energy to resist. Will power creates an obsession for the need to control.

Trying to control your mind to take steps you believe will give you ultimate control is the equivalent of asking a cat not to chase a mouse. It's futile!

Every time you think you are using your willpower to resist temptation, you are giving the temptation more credit than it needs. The dark side of willpower is your rival!

Learn to recognise the thought patterns that keep you continually engaging in the same behaviours – behaviours that can imprison and deceive you into thinking they are adding value to your life.

You are you for a reason, and most importantly you have the potential to be and to do great things, but obsessing on the need to take control of willpower will keep you in a state of misery.

You may feel that if you are able to utilise your willpower, everything will fit into place. This is a myth. Unfortunately, what emerges is a constant sense of failing.

Do you really think that life is supposed to be so difficult? We have the power to change our perceptions No matter what we are going through. We just need to believe in this process of change .

By learning to let go of will power, it will give you the freedom to explore other options and connect with your authentic self too!

Emotional Rollercoaster

Your feelings represent the essence of your soul.
Your feelings are created by your thoughts which
are derived from your past experiences.

Expressing your emotions is one thing, but allowing them to take control of your life, where you don't know whether you are coming or going is another. Sometimes, you need to look towards your future and access your emotional reservoir.

Throughout life, we experience a wide range of emotions. Each emotion can represent the extreme highs and the deep lows we experience. As for the latter – no one is exempt I am afraid. When you feel low you may experience sadness, hurt and anger which is sometimes born out of fear.

Try and reflect on how these emotions manifest in your behaviours. Do you give each of these feelings a permanent parking permit in your emotional territory? Or are you able to appraise each emotion for what it is without allowing it to become who you are? By merely recognising and re-evaluating, you will find you are able to move on.

So many people walk around with emotional baggage and fail to recognise the impact it's having on themselves and how they interact with others. You may have been hurt, but that does not mean you need to stay hurt and continue to hurt others. This is all about choice and change. By all means allow your emotions to be expressed freely – but don't let them take a complete hold of your life to the point of suffocation

You do have the choice! Whether you continue on an exhausted, emotional rollercoaster ride, or step off and take a more relaxing but nonetheless an exhilarating ride.

Frozen Heart

If you have your heart on constant freeze, it's time to switch on the defrost button and begin to experience the abundance of love that is freely available to you.

Don't allow your past experiences to keep your heart from the warmth and love that is waiting to enter into your life! Every breath that you take represents, in spite of the heartache, just how far you have come in life. You may feel alone and sad – longing for your days to pass quickly in an attempt to ease the pain. You may feel that you do not have the ability to love again.

Sensational aches in your heart represent an internal pain that no one seems to be able to touch or relate to. You may feel that this experience will never end and that you will be alone in your sadness.

Thoughts such as 'I am a failure' can become the focal point of how you relate to yourself. This keeps you in a deep freeze; unable to see an alternative and more helpful view about yourself.

You may find yourself waiting and waiting for something new and fabulous to happen, only to be disappointed and frustrated when it doesn't happen. Perhaps you are blissfully unaware that you may be blindly waiting for the wrong something?

Adding value to your life only truly happens when you free yourself from the coldness of any hurt and pain you may have experienced. When you warm up you will naturally begin to love and your live life to its full potential. If you are finding all this difficult (even impossible) to absorb and reflect upon, it may be time to take some time out and communicate with your authentic self.

As night follows day the love will begin to flow freely

within, and your frozen heart will melt slowly away. In essence the more you keep your heart frozen, the more you will continue to be robbed from experiencing a life where love flows freely within you and in turn you will express unconditional love to others.

Sustaining your Strength

Be strong throughout the seasons of your life.
Some seasons stay longer than you would like, so
allow your inner strength to comfort you so that
you will be prepared to deal with the unexpected.

维持强度

Sometimes the situations in your life will be stormy. You may look around and think your situation is worse than the next person. Such perceptions do not help you out of the situation, but keep you stuck in it! An important thing to remember is that you are unique, and therefore somebody else's troubles could never fit the equation to your circumstances and experiences.

17

For the storms to calm down in your life you will have to deal with the rain, extreme heat, and freezing conditions. Remembering this will not only increase your inner strength but also your ability to understand what you are going through; which is the cornerstone to deal with the unexpected. You may ask, "What is inner strength?" Inner strength is the ability to keep on going when you are knocked from all different angles. It is the ability to understand that this is a process in your life you need to reflect and learn from.

Start the process in understanding how you respond and deal with emotional pain, and this will give you a template of how to deal with life's ups and downs. I am not stating that you are going to be smiling when things go wrong in life, but you will have a sense that no matter how severe a situation may seem, no day really last forever!

Your ultimate motto should be is that you do indeed have the inner strength to deal with whatever knocks on your door. You may not like what you are going through; nevertheless you can definitely learn immensely from whatever it is that keeps on knocking. The secret to being victorious in your circumstances is to recognise that your Creator has a master plan, which is about reaping the rewards after experiencing the learning process to what we call LIFE.

Embracing your Uniqueness

There is no such thing as equality. You are unique and therefore not equal to anyone.

Every time you feel that you should be equal or better than another person, you are allowing yourself to fall short of understanding the true essence of being unique.

Living your life to its full potential sometimes means you have to enter some undesirable and unfamiliar experiences. What you achieved yesterday and today are imprints of your inimitable character. Yes, there may be flaws in you which you may eagerly want to erase, but remember this: you are you for a reason. It is therefore your duty to understand the intricate details of your character with the aim of working with what you have, rather than what you wish you had, to the best of your potential.

Trying to live somebody else's life is not only representing a fraud identity but also taking away the one thing that your Creator designed for you – your uniqueness.

Mapping out your circumstances against someone else's is like trying to recreate yourself as the carbon copy of that person.

Whatever experiences you have had in the past; it is now time for you to spend precious moments with the most unique person you will ever encounter, and learn to sit with who you are, so that your true self can emerge. Ask yourself, 'Who am I?' Let your answer reflect your uniqueness and not an image that does not represent your authentic self!

Living with the Unexpected

Learn to live with the unexpected rather than trying to mould it into what you would consider familiar and safe.

Do you stand or fall when you are faced with challenges? It's in our human make-up to feel safe and sound in our comfort zone – in that cozy place where making a decision or taking a risk is not an option because of the discomfort it brings. Unfortunately, there are no guarantees regarding the outcome of life and therefore we will always be living with the unexpected. However, this should not keep you from aspiring towards new things. Every time you worry about something, why not let your Creator take control whilst you take a back seat, take a deep breath and let go of what you are trying to control.

You may say 'I can't'. My message to you is "Yes you can." Maybe it's about time you switched the mute button on the internal voice that says "you can't!"

Accepting the notion that there are some things you will never be able to control enables you to free yourself from always feeling that your life is operated by a set of rules and regulations. Most importantly, 'control' should not even be a concept in your life, because when the inevitable 'unexpected' happens, there will be no 'off' button on your remote control to stop what has already happened.

Live life and ride the storms. But don't forget that you are the one that holds the power to make your life more fulfilling.

Who has really let you down?

Has anyone ever let you down? Or is this your misguided perception?

You may find yourself in a situation where you feel that you have been let down. Perhaps even by the people you love and trust the most, such as family, friends or work colleagues. Before you allow this thought process to continue you need to first ask yourself, "Why am I in this situation?" or "Why do I feel that I have been let down?"

When you reflect on these questions, you may come to the conclusion that in actual fact no-one has let you down! I know you are thinking I may be missing the point. Stick with me!

The reality is that it is your expectations that have let you down – and they will do so time and time again until a different perception regarding feeling let down is adopted.

So the next time you feel that you have been let down, ask yourself "did they really let me down, or have my expectations let me down." Does that mean you should not ask for help from other people? Indeed, we are wired to seek help; however it is when we feel that it is our right to never be let down.

Take note of the types of thoughts that feed this unhelpful assumption. This will help you explore the sequence of your misguided assumptions.

Give and Take

Giving and taking do not necessarily go hand in hand. Your aim should be to give unconditionally and take sparingly.

How do you feel when you have acted out of generosity? Do you only feel completely satisfied when the favour is returned and you gain as much, if not more than you have given?

26

Sometimes we have the misguided belief that we will leave ourselves depleted and therefore must take back in order to re-fill our reservoir. The process of giving can be a rewarding experience when you give from the heart without expecting any return favour.

Now let's move on to the notion of taking! This is something that many people struggle with. By not 'taking back' we might feel we have lost out, and therefore try everything in our power to 'get back' what we think we deserve. Take a moment to reflect on this. Have you ever given someone a gift (either material or emotional) without expecting anything in return? If the answer is 'no' give it a go, all the time asking yourself, "How do I feel?" Perhaps you feel cheated? On the other hand you may feel a thrill and want to give more? The choice is yours.

Greed

Never let greed overshadow what you need. Just because someone else seems to have more of what you think you need than you, it does not mean what they have is right for you.

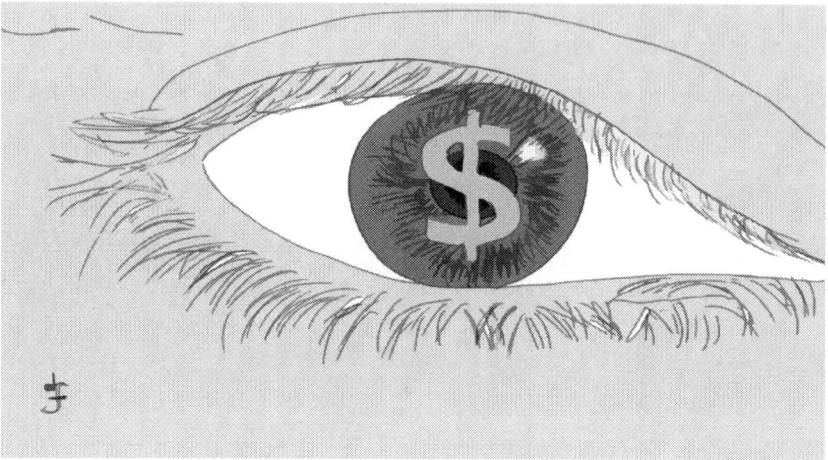

Nothing will come to you before it is time. If you are finding it difficult to focus on what you have you run the risk of becoming envious towards those who you think have more than you. If someone else has a bigger house than you, a better car to drive, or the family you would have liked, you need to ensure you direct any envious feelings into positive ones. Positive envy is healthy. There is absolutely no harm in aspiring to those who have succeeded. The danger is when you feel that you need to reciprocate their life. This has the capability to destroy your own character; but most importantly you begin to adopt one of the most deadly sins – greed and envy.

Greed and envy entraps you from birthing what is rightfully yours.

Protection vs. Rejection

Have you ever experienced rejection after rejection and wondered why this keeps on happening to you?

Consider this: maybe this perceived rejection is really a sign of your creator's protection? Maybe you are being given the message that you are on the wrong path and this is not the path that has been planned for you? Perhaps you are on a path you need to learn from, and then leave behind? Rejection is painful – especially if the pattern keeps on repeating. Rejection leads to a sense of personal failure, and your sense of self-esteem will dip or plummet depending upon how rejected you feel.

Very few people actually understand the real essence of rejection. The thought generally associated with rejection is, "I am not good enough." This leaves us with a terrible sense of being unloved. When we allow these thoughts to ruminate it leads us to behave in negative and often harmful ways. This is called 'acting out', and 'acting out' blindly damages our whole sense of self.

If you are not careful, ruminating on what could or should have been is likely to become the baseline of your thoughts. To prevent this – hold on to this:

If you never experience rejection, what lessons will you learn in life?

Whether you are in a relationship or striving for your desired career path; we are all destined to experience rejection at some point. It's what you do with the rejected feeling that is important.

So next time you experience rejection take a moment and think deeper. Is this really rejection? Or, alternatively, are you being protected and guided towards better things that are waiting to happen in your life? What we think is right for us is not always necessarily good for us in the long run. Take time out and let your Creator continue protecting you, even if the rejection process is overwhelming, your rewards will be worth the agonising wait.

Decision Making

We make most decisions based on our circumstances.What we learn is based on our belief systems at any given time.

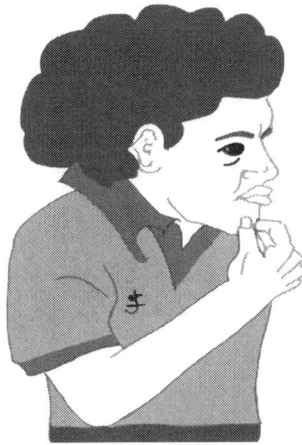

Take a moment to think about the decisions you have made recently.

On reflection would you make the same decisions again?

It is important to note that whatever decisions you make you will never get the same outcome twice. If this was the case you would remain in a time warp where nothing changes. Our experiences and circumstances are continuously changing. Nothing remains stagnant.

In reality, each breath you take represents time evolving continuously. Life is like an escalator, where you go up and down – different people get on and off at different times. Each time every one of us gets on that escalator it is a different moment in time. So despite how many decisions you make, time has moved on and what was right or wrong then will be different now.

So remember this: it is your 'belief system' and not 'your circumstances' that will influence your decision making process and the ultimate outcome.

Stuck in the Wilderness

You may feel lost, directionless, and even helpless in your situation. You may even feel that someone else is to blame for this? A truth worth remembering at this time is that you are not alone.

You are you for a reason. So many people feel that they need to be somebody else – somebody they are not designed to be. If you feel helpless in your current situation, ask yourself the following:

1. Am I feeling lost because I have allowed someone/

something to dictate who I am – to give me

attributes or failings that are not the real truth?

2. Am I feeling alone because I have given up on myself based on what other people have told me, about what I can or cannot achieve?

Helplessness is not a reality – it is a feeling about how you have decided to tackle (or not tackle) your current situation. Living within this state of mind probably feels like the only option you have. Going through tough times with a sense of aloneness engulfing you can be very difficult indeed to cope with, therefore you begin to adopt behaviours and habits that, in essence, are preventing you from experiencing the inner peace and happiness you deserve.

Don't let your pride stop you asking for help. You may feel alone but I can assure you help is out there for the asking.

Do something to make your situation better right now. Talk about what is crippling you. Finding an exit door from your wilderness, so you can begin to really connect with the real world is so very important – and a gift you deserve to allow yourself.

36

Be true to Yourself

Are you emotionally involved with someone (or something) who is robbing you of your self-worth? What seemed right in the beginning does not necessary mean that it is good for you in the long run.

No matter who you are, you are capable of experiencing happiness. You also have the ability to love unconditionally. That said: you should never love foolishly.

To be loved does not mean you have to compromise who you are. The blue print to your identity is your uniqueness and vitality. If you encounter a changing of your emotions, and no longer know whether what you are doing is right or wrong, you have to stop and ask yourself just why you keep on the same track. Have a reality check-in with yourself.

To highlight how important you are to yourself here are a few simple questions.

1.   "Who am I living my life for?"

2.   "What are my values?"

3.   "Am I able to live by them?"

4.   "Am I afraid of expressing who I am to others in fear of rejection?"

There may be many times when people don't understand you or where you are coming from. During these times it is important for you to always go back to basics to be at a place where you begin to really understand yourself.

If reaching your full potential means that you have to be selfish, then so be it.

Remember: When people don't understand you, it is generally highlighting the fact that they simply don't understand themselves.

Problem Solving

On the surface of every problem are a reason and a lesson to be learnt.

Problems are all about building our character. It is a pointless exercise trying to determine the outcome of your problems. You will only become more and more frustrated. Let your problems arise and deal with them accordingly.

What would your life look like if all your problems were

deleted? Would you have an interesting story to tell? Probably not!

Every time you are faced with a situation that feels too much to handle, embrace it and deal with it accordingly – you might just surprise yourself.

There is a solution to absolutely everything, so it is vital that you do not remain stuck in your traffic jam of problems.

Whatever you do, do it well and relish in the satisfaction of being your own problem solver. The more problems you solve the more confident you will become. Frustration will be modified to a level where you no longer feel unsatisfied.

True Knowledge

Your knowledge is your power. The more you absorb, the more empowered you will become.

Think about the following statement.

'Everything that you think you know, in reality, tells you what you don't know.'

Many of us are traveling along a constant conveyer belt trying to figure out what we feel we need to know. Stop for a moment and ask yourself the following questions.

1.   How would you describe the knowledge you have acquired?

2.   Is this knowledge based on a reflection of your true identity?

3.   How do you measure up to who you really are?

4.   How knowledgeable are you about your unique character?

How we absorb knowledge depends on our own unique make-up. You have been created to have a unique character that cannot be replicated – therefore your perception of what you have read or listened to, belongs to you and to you alone!

The next time you feel disempowered by your circumstances take a stand and be proud of the things you know, and remember, each time you encounter a difficulty you add more understanding about how to deal with such difficulty.

It is time to get off the emotional rollercoaster, and

choose a less bumpy (or traumatic) ride, by learning to accept that the only knowledge worth fighting for is the seed your Creator has planted for you to grow.

Share Your Knowledge

Share your knowledge and start the process of universal knowledge.

It should be part of our human nature to pass on our knowledge. You may have vast knowledge, and have experienced a great deal in your life, but if you are holding onto your knowledge in the fear that you will lose a part of yourself you are adopting an attitude that will keep you within an unhealthy mindset.

Learn to feed others with the knowledge that you have acquired. Offer them the opportunity to expand on what you have given them and thus begin the process of universal knowledge.

Some people anxiously feel they have to protect their knowledge because it has taken them so long to acquire it. Worry no more; by becoming part of the universal knowledge chain you will become an important part of creating an environment for people to learn and continue learning. In essence, this will empower you and all those with whom you come into contact.

A Lifetime of Agony

Don't set yourself up for a lifetime of agony based on your frustrations with your circumstances.

The dead certain route to self-destruction is adopting a belief that there is no way out of your situation.

You may feel frustrated with yourself and the things you have continued to do over and over, as well as what you have allowed people to do to you. It's important that you are always in the driving seat regarding what your next move should be. Don't wait on others to negotiate which direction you desire to go; as this will keep you doing the same thing time and time again just like a hamster on a wheel.

By having a firm heart to heart with yourself you begin to recognise that you have the internal tools to fix whatever it is that is keeping you from getting back on track.

A Sense of Helplessness

You may be at a place in your life where you feel that you lack direction leaving you feeling a sense of helplessness.

Just like birds naturally learn to fly – so you too will take off when you decide to stop thinking and start believing that you can. We can fly – We all have the ability to prosper in our lives, but it takes determination as well

49

as having a belief system that you have the ability to succeed regardless of what you think you are going through.

Our positivity needs to filter through the doubt and fear we are harbouring – so we can begin the process of achieving. "I can't do it?" may be the rumination – the constant message that has become set in your mind, keeping you in a self-imposed prison where the walls close in on you.

Do you keep acting out the same habits day in and day out and then wonder why you still remain in the same place as you were yesterday and the day before? STOP. The key to flying is based on two fundamental things.

1.   No matter what you are going through, always give yourself a confidence booster. You may not be perfect in your eyes, but your imperfections are perfect in your Creator's image.

2.   Learn to live with the discomfort of uncertainty rather than trying to control it. You can't control it. Only He can.

Cleanse your Mind

Give your mind a good spring clean. Start by clearing away unwanted thoughts that are blocking your ability to think clearly.

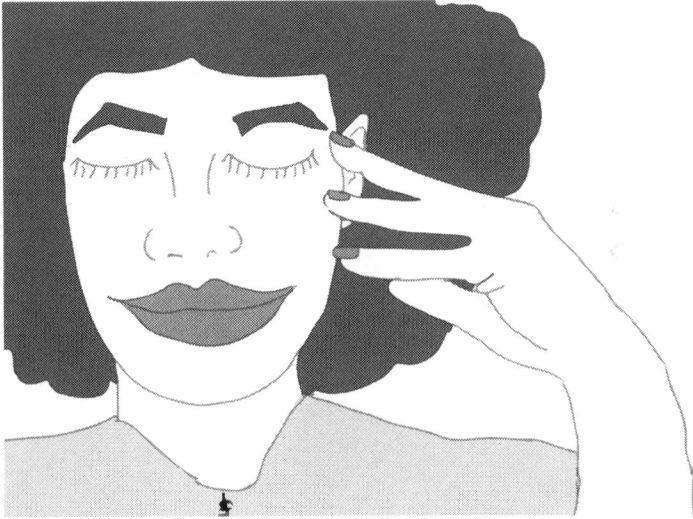

Is your mind like a maze? One minute you think you are on the right track – in tune with your true self. The next minute your thoughts swerve to take you away from the person you really are, and making you feel lost.

The process of cleansing your mind needs to become a

51

habit that you adopt on a daily basis.

Learn to meditate and remain focused on what you are thinking and how you are feeling. Don't run from tricky thoughts that make you feel uneasy about yourself. Deal with negativity as a matter of urgency. It only takes one negative thought to take you on the wrong track where you will come face to face with a dead end, leaving you feeling helpless all over again.

Rise above whatever is keeping you on lock down and creating turmoil in your inner world. You will always be challenged by negative thoughts that will crop up when you least expect them. Nevertheless, the power you have to stay on the right road is bigger than you might think, so banish negativity and do not allow such thoughts to impact on your world and ultimate behaviour.

Walk Away

*Sometimes you just need to make that decision
and walk away to end the pain and anguish.
There may be thunder; but without a doubt,
just as sun follows rain, there will be sunshine
waiting to burst through.*

There will be seasons in your life where you should expect rainfall and even thunder. A time when waking up each morning seems like an unbearable burden. The heaviness of your heart speaks volumes, but at the same time you feel silenced by your immense pain. When we encounter such experiences, we feel so low that looking for that one thing to take you out of these uncomfortable feelings seems impossible.

You may question whether you have the ability to walk away and if you do you fear what the consequences could be. Each long day stretching out ahead appears to signify a life time of misery. When you sense you must walk away from something or someone, you need to hold on to the fact that there is surely more to gain in the long term.

We all have a story to tell. By walking away you will enable yourself to be the author of your own life – a life where, one day, you look back and realise how much you have learnt. Be brave enough to walk in to a place that will not only enable you to have a better quality of life, but also give you the satisfaction that you did what was right for you at that particular time.

Revenge

Experience tells us it is wrong to accept the notion that revenge is sweet. The truth is that the ultimate taste of revenge in the long run is bitterness.

You may be finding that you can't help but reminisce on the hurt that you have experienced (or are still experiencing). You may feel that the only way you can calm your inner turmoil is to get even, so that you no longer feel the pain. Reminders of your pain are ever prevalent, which is why the concept of forgiveness is absent from your daily vocabulary.

You may ask, 'How can I forgive when I am still hurting so much?' This may be a question that you ponder over and over until you feel as if you are going quite insane. By learning the art of forgiveness you begin to adopt an approach to life where you are able to let go and move on. Indeed this does not happen naturally. Instead it takes great faith to begin to understand that you are not destined to grow the seeds of revenge into a forest of bitterness.

Troubled Soul

Every time you feel your bitterness or hate lingering, be aware that this is a sign your soul may have become contaminated. Act now and redirect your soul from an unhealthy emotional state. Soullessness will inhibit your growth.

It's alright to be troubled when unfortunate things happen to you – but something within your surroundings can help you out of this tiresome emotional state. Healthy living starts with nurturing your soul by subtracting all your past painful experiences and holding onto the concept that each day is a new day to let go of the past. You may not feel that you have the capability of being a source of inspiration to yourself, but the more you deny yourself this freedom, the more troubled your soul will remain.

What you have experienced must be filtered into two categories.

1.   Things that fed my soul in the past.

2.   Things that destroyed my sense of self.

This division will enable you tap into the things that will help you when you are in trouble. It will also give you an account of how much time and energy you give to the empty elements that are draining the goodness from your soul. Every morning check in with yourself

.

1.   How much positive energy do you have to inspire yourself, as well as others?

2.   That you are not allowing a bitter taste to destroy

the sweetness that you deserve to experience.

Don't be Ruled by Greed

It is not money, but people's greed, that creates problems. Greed can overshadow the true blessings that money can add to one's life.

What is the characteristic of greed? Think hard—does having money actually constitute greed? So many of us are led to believe that money is the root of evil, but think again.

So many people in the world today base their identity on the monetary wealth they have accrued. But the other side of this coin is that we should not be afraid of being wealthy.

Consider the following;

1.   Who are you without your wealth?

2.   Who are you with your wealth?

3.   How much has either having or not having wealth ruled or overshadowed who you perceive yourself to be.

4.   Do you base your sense of self and credibility on the state of your wealth?

If you begin to refer to your character based on how much money you have (or how much you might have), you have not truly recognised your other potential gifts. What you have adopted is a belief system that your wealth is bigger and better than what your Creator has developed within you. This is unhealthy.

Unanswered Questions

You're not in it to win it; you are merely here to experience it.

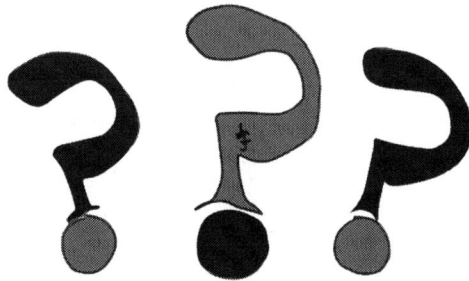

The inexorable will always happen, leading you to feel emotionally empty or lost. A belief may evolve about you having to find the solution for unanswered questions. "Why me?" will be the continual cry as you search for answers.

Annoying as it might be, no matter who we are, or what

we have experienced, there are just some things in life that cannot be explained in simple and acceptable terms.

During these periods you will undoubtedly benefit from having a one to one, a session communicating with your Creator. You may not always get the answer that you want; but what you will get are the solutions that you need and which are right for you.

Sometimes it feels as if the unforeseen has knocked on your door, gained entry, and barged in leaving you shocked and at a loss as to what to do because of the sudden unexpectedness. This may leave you feeling misplaced and searching in all the wrong places for the right answers.

Try and accept that in these situations your Creator knows best, and that all we need to do is to allow His work to manifest within us.

Gossoholic

Do you find yourself gossiping unnecessarily? If what you say adds nothing positive to a person's life, then delete it from your vocabulary. Don't let your negative words be a part of destroying someone's self-worth or identity.

If it's not worth saying simply don't say it. Never underestimate the power of words!

Every waking hour we use words to express our state

of mind, but when our vocabulary contains words of bitterness or 'put-downs' we are aiding and abetting a robbery of another human being's sense of self-worth.

Why do you do this? Question the motives that drive you to take part in this insidious side of human nature. Are you copying others? Is your life so unhappy that you want others around you to feel worse than you? These are questions worthy of your reflection.

No matter how much you may feel the compulsion to express your opinion, if it is based on you dissecting someone's self-identify, and then you are no better than your words.

In essence, you run the risk of becoming part of what you may dislike in another person. Learn to appreciate, or at least tolerate, the imperfections in others – so that they too can learn to see your short falls for what they are, rather than as a default in your character. Often we have to peer behind bad behaviours to see the goodness in the authentic person standing before us.

Forward Thinking

Some people will use and abuse you and take what does not belong to them. Don't become angered. Instead, take a step back. From this vantage point you will be able to watch and learn from their mistakes. You will also be setting a good example for others willing to see the light.

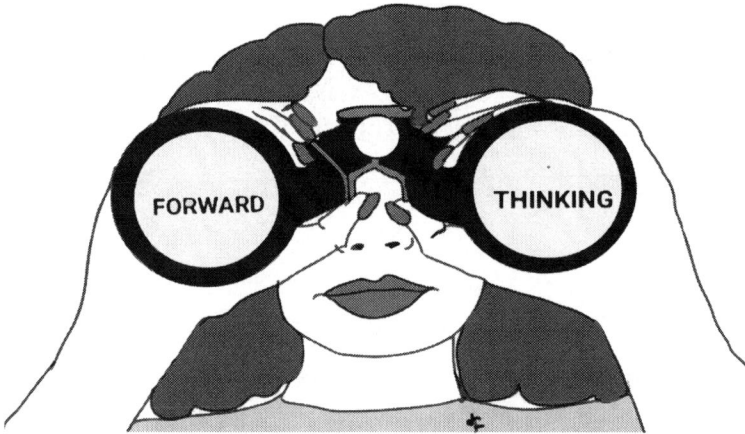

People only get away with what you allow. So when you feel hurt, don't feel you need to hurt them right back. Maybe you need to reflect on why you feel so let down? This reflection will be an invaluable lesson and one that leads you to make changes in how you feel, think, and behave. You will also hurt less.

The time has come for you to stand up for yourself and say, "No more!" Stop the record that's stuck in the groove, endlessly repeating, "why me" over and over again. You do not have to be a victim of your circumstance all your life. You need to know you are victorious in all the things you have achieved, and as you go forward you will be able to learn from your trials and errors.

Allow your inner voice to filter through your heart to enable you through the sticky moments. Learn from those who have hurt you. They may not be in a place where they are able to recognise the consequences of their actions. Most importantly, you will not act on, but deflect, with both a wisdom and understanding that demonstrates maturity and humility.

No longer will you be a part of their unresolved issues – but a separate and complete entity where independency has replaced the sickness of dependency.

Time Out

There are times in your life when you need to take time out to reflect on what you are doing. If you sense someone or something is sapping your energy you must find a way to modify or eliminate this negativity.

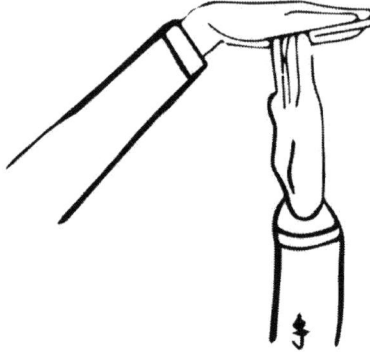

From time to time it is healthy to stop, listen and learn. This will rid you of the 'stuck' feeling that prevents you from moving to the next level of your life.

You cannot buy time!

When you have the frustrating feeling that there is not enough time in your day to complete important tasks for yourself be careful not to miss vital signs that you are working at a pace which has not been designed for you.

If you continue along this insidious path, where you are not in tune with your mind and body, you face the risk of losing your sense of self. Running a race that you should never have started is all too common, and focus on the negative tends to become the topic of discussion instead of what is really important. You will end up exhausted – or even worse – burn out altogether. Then you are of no use to anyone, let alone yourself.

Taking time out can save your soul. Find yourself a protected space that is personal to you. At first your mind will resist this new way of nurturing yourself. Take this time to be still and you will be amazed how good you will feel as a result. There is nothing better than sitting with that feeling of self-satisfaction within your own personal space. All you have to do is give yourself permission.

Fear

Stop hiding behind fear. Worrying about what might happen, only serves to keep you adrift at sea.

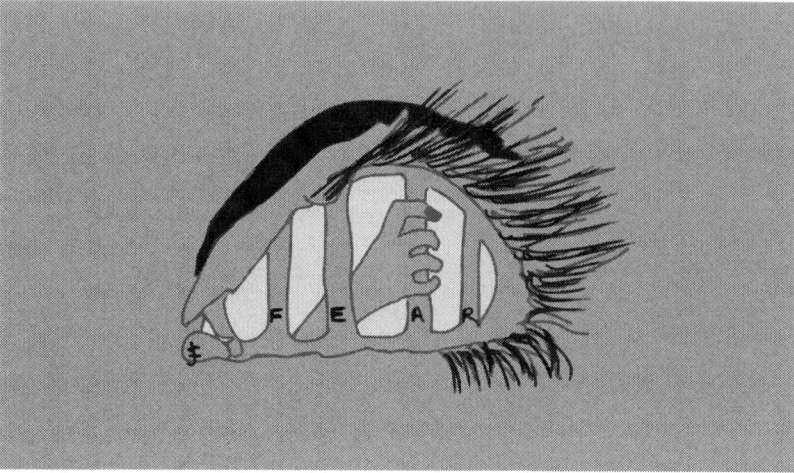

Fear's acronym is—False Evidence that Appears Real.

The truth is that your fears are never real. Instead they are mythical anticipations of what could happen, not what has or will happen.

70

Although fear is based on false evidence, it nevertheless has a disabling effect on a person's life. Overcoming fear is based on your ability to appraise what you are going through with a new level of understanding. You no longer need to feel suffocated by your unhelpful thoughts. Such thoughts will tell you that "you can't". Did you know the word "can't" is in fact a negative word? It gives the message that you are unable to achieve something? Start by deleting "can't" out of your vocabulary – as nothing is impossible!

Most importantly you are not destined to be a prisoner of your fear. This knowledge in itself is very powerful indeed.

The Road Is Not Easy

*At times you may feel that walking away will
solve all of your problems. This is too simplistic.
For most of us the road map to our lives is not
as straight and clear as we would like but filled
with pot-holes and hair-pin bends.*

It is inevitable that we will experience sharp bends
and fall into pot holes along our journey of life. The
magnitudes of your problems that manifest are based
on how you perceive and deal with such problems. Take

a moment to reflect and ask yourself how you deal with situations that happen unexpectedly. Are you the type of person that no matter how much positive energy is swirling in the air, you tend to form an alliance with the opposition – the negativity?

Do you find yourself asking – "Why am I never successful? Why do I always seem to get the bad luck?" I am sorry to have to say this; but you are the antagonist in your life story and the main reason why you remain in your current state of negativity.

It is likely you are so immersed in your way of thinking that all you think you can do is attract the same things in your life that keep you on that same road with all the pot holes. Life's road is not an easy one to travel along. No-one said it should be. However, if time and time again, you reach the same pot hole it's time to swerve and study the road map a while before you choose a path that enables you walk on before turning to look back and reflect. Even further along the road you will find yourself learning valuable lessons from your mistakes. This is so much more satisfying than reaching another road block!

Better Days to Come

You may feel that your pain is deeper than anything you could ever have imagined. Allow your pain to manifest itself, but not to reside and take hold of your existence.

When we feel physical pain, most of us immediately reach for a brand of pain killers to numb this feeling so that we can function with our everyday issues. This is not so when we experience a wrenching pain in our hearts, and a numbness in our souls. Words are unable to describe the intensification of such feelings; which in itself can leave you feeling silenced and isolated from everyone and everything.

You may ask "how on earth did I reach this point where my emotions have overwhelmed me and overtaken my sense of well-being and sense of self?" Perhaps every emotional 'quick fix' you've tried has failed to do the job of making everything alright? How empowering to know that, in reality, your cure for such pain is to let go and release yourself.

Try and take a moment to write down the things that need to happen for you to experience Take Control of your Tomorrow. Cross out the ones over which you have no control, such as those that require someone else to change their behaviour. Rank the rest in order of what you are able to cope with right now. Then begin to slowly work through whatever is preventing you from moving on, step by step, at your own individual pace.

Simplification is the key

*Nothing in your life should be complicated. You
honestly hold the keys to a simple life*

One of your main goals in life should be to simplify things
that appear complicated. In every situation always take
on board the following notion, that there is 'possibility'
waiting in the wings to jump out and challenge what
you think is impossible.

The grass always seems greener on the other side of life

– the truth of the matter is that it is not greener – it is just different.

Try to live life to its full potential. Subtract from your personal space all the things that are not adding any value to the desires that you have for yourself.

Life does not have to be complicated at all. Grab the keys of life and unlock your potential so that you can do what is right for you.

Unlock your Love

Can you locate the love within you? If the answer is "no" you must read on – because as soon as you can locate it a new way of expression will guide you to a place where you can begin to love unconditionally.

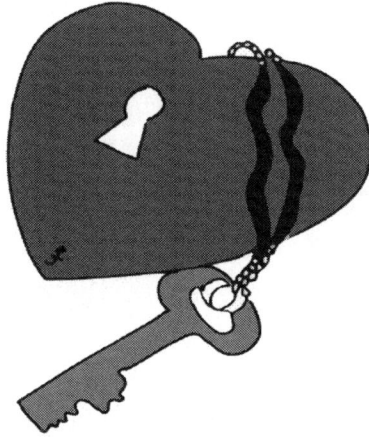

When love knocks on your door what do you do? How many times have you carried past hurt into new and potentially good relationships?

To be able to love unconditionally and unselfishly is indeed a skill. It is something that, first and foremost, needs to be nourished within you. If you are forever reminiscing on what went wrong in the past and feel that you are the victim of your circumstance, it will prove difficult for you to unlock your potential to love and be loved.

It can take time to pull yourself back together when you have been hurt. A broken heart finds it difficult to trust again and experience potential good loving. You may only be able to recall experiences where you were treated unfairly and then this becomes the starting point for your future relationships. This is the point where so many people get stuck – sometimes paralysed with fear of the same thing happening all over again.

When relationships don't quite work out, and you keep questioning why this should be? Maybe you have built an emotional wall around you. A wall designed to keep you safe but in reality blocks your true feelings and stifles true expression of emotions.

When love knocks on your door, welcome it. One thing is for sure, although you have experienced what it's like to feel unloved, by unlocking your love you are potentially allowing yourself to experience a new vibrant love that is worth holding on to.

Stop and Listen to your Heart

Listen to your heart. It will never let you down.
Allow it to function to the very best of its ability.

By taking two steps back to reflect on where you are heading you will take yourself to a vantage point where the view will be enlightening.

Tell me.....

1.   How much energy are you investing in your vision?

2.   Do you need to take time out to reflect on where you are going and if you are traveling in the right direction?

3.   Is the plan going to be straight forward? Or might you find traps and cracks that were not originally in your plan?

Regardless of the process of your journey, if you have a clear vision and an attitude of 'anything is possible', it is unlikely that you will be side tracked for too long as you will see the cracks and swerve round them. It's about having your eyes wide open.

Everyone is entitled to have a vision that will enable them to create something new. Therefore it's vital that you take stock of the various aspects of your life and look ahead to a future, where your mind, body and soul are in sync with each other.

Cleanse your Heart! If you're holding onto something that doesn't bring joy in to your life it may be time to have a heart detox so that you no longer feel the need to re-live the darker side of your life.

Imagine if your heart was to stop functioning every time you felt bitterness or anger towards someone – how scary is that!

The physical function of the heart is to keep the flow of blood regulated. We take in oxygen and expel carbon dioxide – but how do you regulate the emotions of the heart? What do you take in and what do you get rid of?

Do you tend to digest things in an unhelpful way? Do you find it hard to forgive because you are hurting? Each time you allow bitterness and hate to have a continuous flow through your heart, you are also infiltrating your mind, body and soul.

Holding on to bitterness and hatred puts a barrier up and stops you seeing things for what they really are, leading to your self-awareness and vision of others becoming distorted.

One may have all the external trimmings of a Beauty Queen or a Handsome King, but a sense of internal and external mismatch confuses the true reflection and a barrier is built between the false and authentic self. Seek the truth, and the next time you feel the presence of bitterness or hate filtering through your words or behaviour, take note that it is probably time to give your heart a good tender loving MOT.

Give Credit

You can't take credit for your existence, but you can take ultimate credit in how you react to your circumstances.

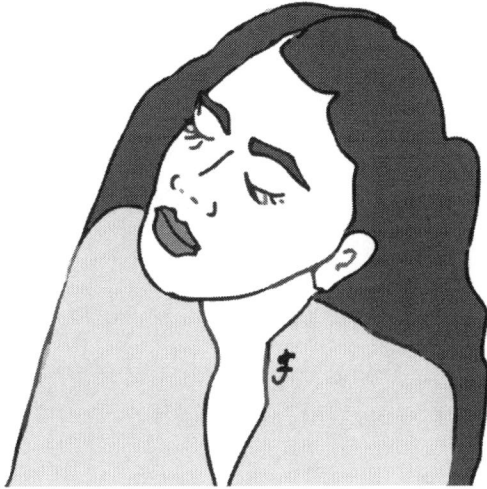

How do you come to terms with what is important in your life?

When do you think you'll reach the point where you can say, "Okay, I've done as much as I can and now it's time for my Creator to take the lead?"

85

The more you push the compulsion to be the one who is the sole driving force of your accomplishments to accomplish, the less you are able to learn the true essence to life. Learn to look beyond the unexpected. Allow your Creator to manage any internal conflict that you may be experiencing.

Indeed you do have every right to feel exhausted by your experiences. Yet by the same token you owe it to yourself not to lapse into a state of hopelessness, where you keep feeding your internal self with an unnecessary internal battle.

Become a lifelong seeker of living, and learn from the blessings that your Creator has given you. Search within your spiritual self for answers. I can assure you – all the tools you need are locked within the unique you.

How wonderful it will feel when you experience this state of confusion changing and you can begin to take control of how you wish to react to your circumstances – as this gives a reflection of just how credible you are.

Internal Love

There is no greater love than your own. Locate it from within so that you can release it.

Love will often let you down – this is the nature of the beast – this is the risk we take when we love.

To be loved is a natural desire and often overwhelming.

However, if you have not located the loving within you, it should not be surprising that you are not attracting it from others. Instead you will undoubtedly fall into the trap of searching endlessly for love you desire from others, all the time failing and wondering why? "What is wrong with me?" you may cry, as your heart remains lost and lonely.

When you think people have let you down, you may well need to think again. Perhaps the answer lies in the fact that you have not mastered the art of loving yourself, and are yet to locate and unlock the love within you.

It's time to stop the frantic search. It's time to begin loving the lovable you!

Whatever you may believe – and in spite of your past experiences – you have as much right as the next person to give and receive love – so begin the process of loving right now. You will be amazed how loved up you will begin to feel.

Grow and Learn

*Every problem you encounter is an opportunity
for you to grow and keep on growing. Undeniably
you will rise again but first you must learn from
your falls.*

Learn to nourish the seeds that your creator has planted
in your life. Each time you stumble upon a situation
which leaves you feeling uneasy, ask yourself "is there

something I can learn from this experience?" No matter how much you feel affected or defeated you are not isolated. There will always be someone, or something, that will give you the kick-start that you need to enable you to grow in the midst of adversities.

Contrary to what you might have been told, we are all destined for great things. However, this can only materialize when you start to believe that you can and will achieve. You may not be where you want to be right now, but this does not mean you can't get to where you need to be one day soon. Ignite your faith so that it can start working for you.

*The way you handle your success will determine
the longevity of the success.*

Gbẹhin aseyori

Yoruba translation

Success is a subjective experience.

Only you can determine how successful you are going to
be in the things you do. Some people believe that success
is based on monetary wealth. This is a sad reflection on
society today.

The importance of being successful is for you to stand

up for what you believe in, even when others cannot see your vision or share your dreams; you keep on striving and believing.

The road to success may not be easy. It was never meant to be easy. But the end product can show you how victorious you are in reaching your God given potential.

Avoid being disillusioned by your success.

To keep on being successful you need to be cautious about how you relate to yourself and others as you go about your business. You need to be in a position where you increase the longevity of your success.

So let your dreams no longer be a figment of your imagination, but a reality that will go on for an eternity.

Misconceptions about Relationships

The mistake people make in their relationships lie in their lack of communication with each other. Don't expect telepathy to add richness to your relationship – it doesn't work that way.

Fact: The break down or survival of relationships is based on how you relate to one another and how you demonstrate your thoughts and needs.

If you feel you are not communicating effectively you

must re-learn the art of communication all over again, just as you might need to re-feed yourself – the roots go right back to babyhood and communication in its simplest form – to learn to talk.

Learning this art will break down all sorts of barriers. Conversations from previous relationships won't work in the new one. You are now embarking on a new relationship and therefore a totally new experience.

Many couples who are reaching the end of their tether feel that they have given their relationship their 'best shot'. They tell themselves that the only way to resolve the difficult times is to end what they once believed was sacred and forever.

Stop, listen, and learn from the communication breakdown that you are both experiencing. Go deeper than you ever have before to try to find some reconciliation. If you are able to reflect together, then the potholes in your relationship can be filled with an attitude that 'all will be well'. Throwing in the towel is so easy, but trust me, communicating your needs effectively is not as difficult as you may think.

A huge misconception is the belief that you can change

or mould your partner into what you want them to be. Next you may 'blame' them because you feel they have let you down. Unfortunately, in these circumstances, the only person that has let you down is you! Your inability to recognise that it is not about changing people but more about understanding and accepting your partner's strengths and weakness' instead of criticizing their inadequacies.

Expectations

It's your expectations, not people that let you down. The less you draw your own expectations from others the less disappointed you will be.

WRONG WAY!

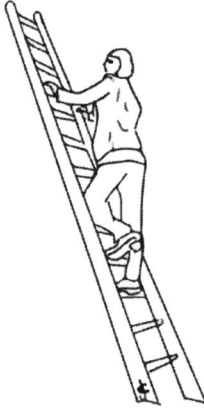

Trying to climb a ladder that is not your own is where you begin to lose the battle to reach your destination.

Reflect and question if you are happy with where you are now?

If, for whatever reason, you are still climbing the same

96

ladder to self-destruction, then maybe it's time to take a few steps back and ask yourself why you are heading in this particular direction.

Maybe you are living your life through the eyes of someone else's dream and their expectations. If so, it is time for you to stop living this way, as all you are doing is stripping yourself of your own personal autonomy. It is time to get back to basics once more.

Next time you feel you have been let down by someone other than yourself, take a look in the mirror and accept responsibility. Once the responsibility is your own then your blurred vision will lift and you will be in control of what it is you really want from your life.

Quick Release

Just as a painkiller gives quick release from physical tension, so forgiveness relieves you from somebody else's emotional baggage-which you have been carrying around for too long.

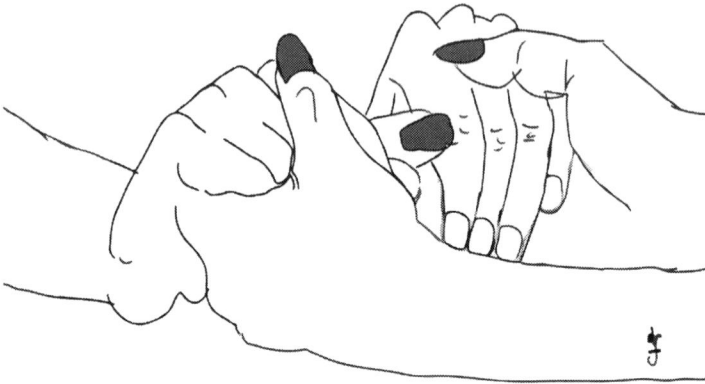

At the heart of all our experiences is a reason.

You may feel an overwhelming compulsion to let the person who has left you feeling emotionally unstable know how much they have hurt you.

Without a doubt we are all entitled to express our pain, but it's important that we adopt the habit of letting go, enabling us to move on down the road without heavy emotional baggage to slow us.

Sometimes carrying someone else's emotional baggage within our heart leaves us with unhealthy thoughts that essentially keep us stuck in a quagmire of unforgiveness.

So the next time you feel a heaviness within ask yourself how much of this is about you or how much is about your inability to let go of something that is really someone else's problem.

Breaking Through – You are not Alone

Whatever you are experiencing learn to adopt the mentality that you are not alone and you will manage to break through eventually.

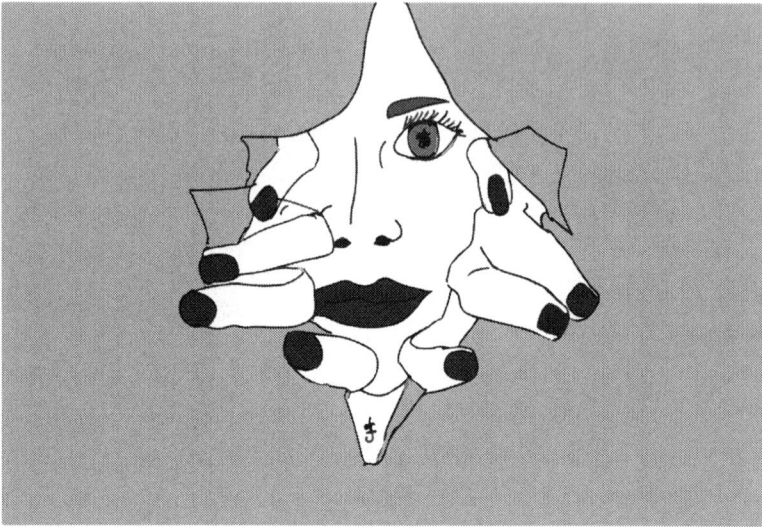

Have you ever studied the behaviour of mice? Although they can be annoying creatures, they will, nevertheless, do almost anything to get to where they want to go. They will change their body shape to fit through the tiniest of pipes. Some are able to beat every mouse trap that is put before them. They have mastered the art that they need to keep going regardless of what obstacles are put in front of them.

Inevitably, we will all face hidden traps and sometimes these traps may keep us on lock down. But we do, as human beings, have the choice to keep on going...and going and break through, or to give up when the going gets tough. This is the ultimate difference between success and failure! It is during the hard times that we must master our next escape route!

You may need to take a different path from the one that got you trapped the first time around. Whatever is at the forefront of your mind you need to adopt the notion that in every situation you encounter, you have the master plan to break through. Remember – your problems are NOT bigger than you. So there is no excuse. You just need to keep pressing towards your desired goals in life and not give up on what could be a good thing.

Irreplaceable

You may think that a precious loss is irreplaceable. Try to learn from your losses and then move on to find something new in your life. When we lose something or someone, it is not necessarily the end of our world, but rather an opportunity to experience something new.

There may be times when you will experience immense pain that cannot be translated into words. Whether this is losing someone through death or the break-up of a relationship, at the forefront of your mind, you may not be able to imagine replacing the experience you had with these people. Experiencing loss can leave you feeling empty and numb. One important concept to hold is that you cannot replace what is lost. If you believe the loss can be recovered you will be forever trying to fill a void in your life. First you grieve and then give yourself the time to heal. ONLY THEN CAN YOU MOVE ON.

During these difficult times it is important to know that it is okay to grieve and release your immense pain – know that it is vital you allow yourself the time to heal. When we lose things in our lives it may be the end of a chapter, but it also hails an opportunity to experience something new. The concept that 'all will be well' can only manifest when you allow yourself a sense of well-being, and adopt a way of life that enables you to live through this experience and come out the other end.

This can only happen if you truly believe that you deserve to be free from your pain.

Listen to your Internal Voice

The more you deny your inner voice, the more you are denying your authentic self. What people see does not necessarily reflect who you are.

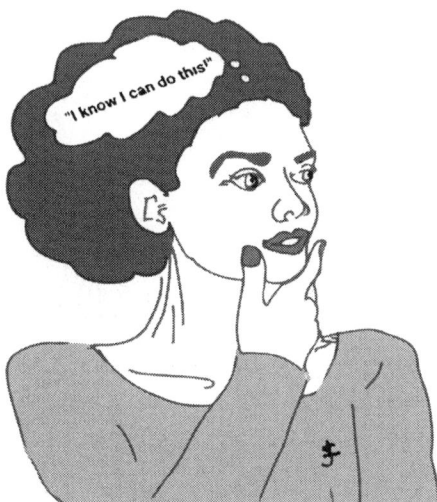

Who you are is simple. It is who you desire to become that complicates things. One of the main rules in life is to listen to your inner voice. Very few people nowadays have the ability to do this but the more we search for our inner voice the more accessible it becomes.

At times when we are faced with an internal dilemma, we may be unsure which voice is directing us in the right way – which one to trust. I call these the Spiritual and the Earthly voices. The latter is what we deal with on a day to day basis. From making the decision when we should get out of bed, to what clothes we should wear.

Our spiritual voice is often the most silent and difficult to hear. If you are not spiritually in tune with yourself it is unlikely you will encounter your spiritual voice. The next time you find yourself in a situation where you are unsure of what to do or where to turn, when every decision you make is unsatisfactory and you can find no peace within yourself, take a moment and listen to the conflicting internal voices. With practice you begin to experience what I term your true spiritual voice – the honesty.

Many of us have formed habits based on our past experience. These habits have somehow shaped our character. So in essence some people have become accustomed to forming an identity that is not truly representative of their authentic self. Whether we like it or not, we tend to be less than honest with ourselves.

How we can undo this and change is based on our ability to strip away the layers that we have formed over the years. In order to set ourselves free and become more in tune with the voice that knows our true existence we must practice hard. The more we try the more successful we will be.

Connecting with your Highest Thoughts

Aim to connect with your highest level of thinking. At this level you will achieve success and satisfaction that would have once seemed impossible.

There will be times when you lose connection and sight of who you are. You may also wonder what your higher thoughts are, and indeed, how you could recognise such thoughts. A higher level of thinking does not happen in moments when you are feeling cluttered in your mind or when you are unsure what it is that you really want from life.

By having an internal dialogue with yourself, you can try to capture new thoughts that might help to take you out of the moments where you feel there is no way out. Focus hard on chasing away unhelpful thoughts and free up a mental space to be filled with positive visualisation. Now you will begin to take control of what you entertain in your thought process. Once you have learnt the art of capturing thoughts that add immense value to you, you will begin to see that there are always possibilities hiding behind the impossible.

Darkness

When darkness lifts from your life, it provides an opportunity for the light to shine through.

Sometimes we may feel that our internal world is full of darkness. Indeed, this will happen to all of us at some time. During these difficult times it is important to protect your mind and check your thoughts. The more we feed our emotional world with negativity, the more our thinking will become clouded and heavy.

Check in with how you think about tricky events. Are you able to think clearly at this time? Are you allowing yourself the time to heal and recharge?

Try not to keep yourself locked away within a thought process that is keeping you from seeing a way out. It is so important to experience a sense of some light being at the end of the tunnel.

When your mind tells you there is no possibility of anything positive coming into your life you must challenge it — only then can you have a happier outcome where you feel in control of your emotions and subsequent behaviour.

It is very difficult, if not impossible, to do this alone. We come into the world alone and we leave alone, but whilst alive we need others. In order to exit this insidious mode of darkness and head towards true enlightenment, you must surround yourself with people who have the capacity to understand you and have the ability to constructively challenge you whilst offering unconditional love or care. Once you begin to understand what has taken you to this dark space you can begin to learn new techniques to take you through the tunnel where your light will not only be your guide but also the part of your destiny.

You as You are

If people can't take you as you are, then be wise and hold back from giving your all. Save your energy for people who are not afraid of you being you and accepting you unconditionally.

Reflect for a moment on what you would consider to be an accurate description of your character. This takes time so don't feel rushed.

Think about whether these ideas about you are based on your own interpretations, or what others have said? Have you been the victim of labeling?

It should come as no surprise when the majority of your interpretations of your self are based on what you have been told by others who claim to know you better than you do. What is fact and what is fiction? What is your reality and what is your fantasy? How do you conduct yourself and live by these inaccuracies?

Too often we allow others to tell us what we can achieve based on their very own inadequacies – they are not ours at all, but have simply been projected on to us. The best thing you can do is throw them right back where they belong! At times this phenomenon happens on a purely unconscious level, but you, nevertheless, need to find the strength to stand up for the authentic YOU and all that that YOU believe in.

Too long we live under the shadow of what someone has told us – that we are incapable of achieving and extending our capabilities.

Think about this: Is there just one thing you would like to achieve? What might that be? Write it down so that you don't forget. Then share it with one or two people and watch their reactions closely. Some may fully back you no matter how unachievable your goal may seem to them, whilst others will see things very differently and throw you a negative attitude.

This doesn't mean they are necessarily bad people. It simply shows you where they are in relation to their achievements – not yours! You are you for a reason and it's this individuality that needs to be owned, expressed and then deeply admired.

Blessings in Disguise

Work with and around your mistakes. It's not about having good days and bad days.

Every day is a blessing – even though sometimes it is in heavy disguise. There are lessons to be learnt from each day of your life.

Contrary to belief, you have never really failed at anything. You might not believe this to be a truth, but try to embrace this concept. Since the day you were born you have been learning along the way. Failure symbolises that you have given up – and giving up means that life no longer exists. So as long as you have life, the motto to chant is, "keep on going".

Perhaps you feel that you have made the same mistakes time and time again, leaving you today feeling unsure which way to turn. This is such a difficult space to find yourself in, and one where many give up on hope. The answer is not necessarily about taking a different route to your decision. It is more about taking a back seat in the experience and taking a mental note of what you are going through – all the while telling yourself "all will be well". Try approaching problems you encounter with the inner dialogue that you might be falling down but you'll get up again and grow and learn from these difficult times.

Most importantly adopt the notion that there is always a reason and a season in everything that you encounter.

Magical Moments

Pull some tricks out of your sleeve. You are totally gifted beyond your imagination. Whatever happens, make each moment magical.

Every step you take – every move you make – whether backwards or forwards, is a motion that simply cannot be frozen in time. Your highest gift is life: everything we do and experience enables us to nourish and nurture this gift.

There may be times when you will feel that things are slipping through your hands quickly, thus giving you the illusion that your world is falling apart. The truth of the matter is that nothing ever really falls apart in anyone's lifetime. Instead, the episodes that occur are part of a journey that gives us the window of opportunity to recognise our uniqueness. It is therefore our duty to capture all those special magical moments, no matter how insignificant, and give our life story the justice that it deserves.

You may say "what is magical about my life." The mere fact that you are reading this signifies that you are searching for something to better your life, which in itself tells you that you do indeed value the gift of life.

Multitude of Angels

Everyone has a multitude of angels at their beck and call. The question I ask is, "Have you connected with yours?" Only when you have made this connection will you realise that you are not alone.

No matter what you are going through at this precise moment you are not alone. Someone somewhere is going through something similar or worse. But you, like everyone else, have the right to express yourself in your own sadness. That said; it's important not to dwell there too long. The time will come to move on.

There may have been times in your life when you have met people who bring something magical into your arena. It may not immediately appear this way, but nevertheless, they have enabled you to deal with a situation when it seemed impossible. We all have angels in our lives; they are there when we are sad and they are also present during happy times. They help us get through one situation to the next. They enable us to breathe every day and give us fuel to keep on living. Your angels are unique. They are based on your individualized needs as well as your belief system and ultimate faith you have in your existence.

"So how can I connect to my angels", you may ask? The answer is simple. You need to reconnect with your real self. Then you can begin subtracting all the insidious and damaging messages that state you are not guided by a higher power. To allow your physical self to be protected and guided by your spiritual self.

Time to be Thankful

Whatever your state of your mind, the one thing you need to hold onto is an attitude of thankfulness – as being connected with what you have demonstrates inner happiness.

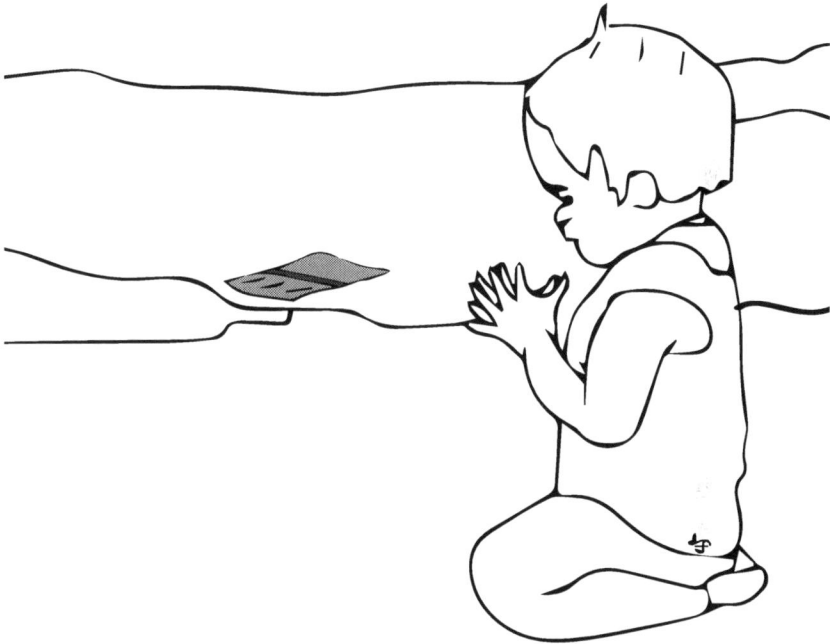

You may feel that the mountains in your life are getting steeper and steeper. You find yourself constantly questioning whether you have enough in you to make it to the top – or to where you want to be. Only to realise that when you reach your destination you begin searching for yet another goal – a dream bigger and better than the last one. What would it take for you to:-

1.   Appreciate what you have?

2.   Stop running a race that's not your own?

No matter what you are going through today, despite how little you think you have, take the time to be thankful. This can be a hard task. You may ask of yourself, "What have I got to be thankful for when you don't feel that you are getting anywhere?"

It is an understandable concept that 'there is always someone who has more than the pittance that you believe you have'.

Unfortunately, what others have is not meant for you. It is what you have that is meant for you, so when you begin to appreciate what you do have, you will recognise that life is not that bad after all.

Unstoppable You

Today is the day that you are not going to stop just because someone questions your capability. Only you should decide whether you want to stop. So start your day with the premise that nothing is going to stop you reaching your desired goals.

Wondering what direction to take can leave you feeling a little confused at times. Try not to get caught up in your own mental traffic jam which keeps you in a whirl of indecision.

Decisions should never be based on your shortcomings. Instead, the path you take must have vision of the future based on your sense of being able to achieve. Too often, when others remind us of our shortcomings, we dwell on their words without question; not only in our minds, but also in our everyday interactions and behaviours.

You may be scared (terrified, even) of grasping a new challenge that takes you out of your comfort zone. Your fear will be taking you prisoner. Fear is the enemy – it has the potential to rob you of so much, depleting you of vital energy as well as altering your perception of the meaning of life.

Whatever you are going through today, hold on to the concept that you are now on the right road and have become the unstoppable you.

Power

You have the power to change your behaviour, but you don't have power to change someone else's.

To begin this process you will first need to be thankful for what you have. Just sit with this concept for a moment – what do you have in your life for which you are truly grateful?

Now imagine that you are in the driving seat of your life. No-one else is driving you! Think about this: Today you got out of bed and chose to read this book. Now apply this same mentality to enable you to put your life back on track.

You may hold the view that before you can become empowered there are certain things (or people!) in your life that you need to change.

But the truth is that in order for you to accomplish what may seem impossible, you need to recognise that you have the potential to bring out the positive in everything you feel, think, and do. By changing your perception you will empower and enable yourself to recognise that waiting for other people to change is not only unhelpful, but also nonproductive.

Feelings of powerlessness are inevitable if you continue to allow others to dictate your potential. How this happens is based on what you have allowed people to add to or take away from your life without your authentic consent. Too often the things you have been told end up becoming the blue print of how you move forward, and you will be stuck within your perceived inadequacies. It should come as no surprise that you will have great difficulty in feeling empowered if you allow someone else's power to crush you.

Now get busy shifting the focus of the power. Understand that you have power – you always did – you just didn't know it. You can change, and it's up to you to start the ball rolling.

Survival of the Fittest

Every breath you take represents how much you are surviving.

At times you may feel that you are drowning in a river of problems where everything seems just too much to deal with. Unfortunately, what often impacts this misery is that we tend not to reach out for help because of an adopted and misguided belief that you can't be helped or that you don't deserve such help. This is terribly sad. Constant unhelpful thoughts make you feel deflated. You stand in your battlefield, lacking hope, and feeling that you are so alone that you almost disappear into the undergrowth. When your state of mind has been feeding you with a defeatist attitude for what seems forever, your ability to extend beyond this defeatist attitude gets harder and harder. Secrets and lies that have become a part of your yesterday are being lived out today and if you don't watch out they will control all your tomorrows.

Try with all you might to hold on to the concept that you no longer have to be a victim of your circumstance. Be victorious about the battles you have won – for we have all won some battles. Go on–give yourself the recognition you deserve. Give yourself a break.

Take Control of your Perceptions

When darkness comes don't be afraid. No matter what, there will always be a flicker of light in your tomorrow to evaporate your darkness enabling you to live a brand new day.

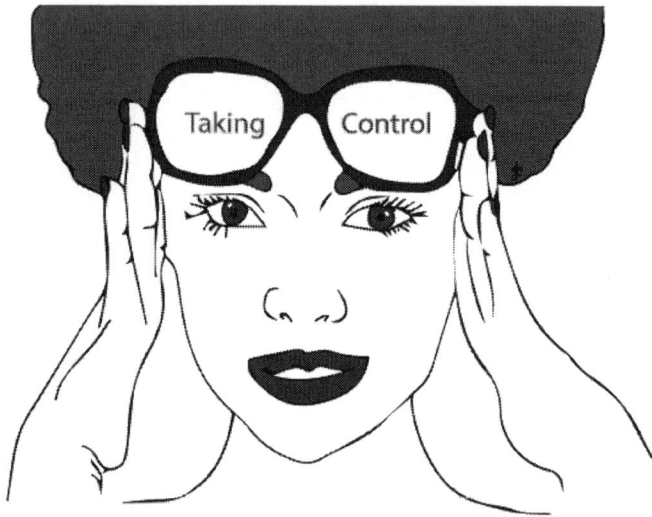

Experience a brand new day with the concept that the changes in your life are stepping stones towards your destiny. You may feel that the weakness in your heart out weighs the lightness of your soul. Try to let go of the things that you feel you need to control.

130

There are always opportunities waiting to enter your world so that you can experience Take Control of your Tomorrow. We all tend to tell our stories through the eyes of pain. This seems to be part and parcel of the way we humans operate. But hear this; there is always another side to the story.

Start today to conceptualise that life is one big story with many elements. You may feel you are being pushed sideways, up and down steep hills, back and forwards and round and round – all your emotions twisted and tangled. The process can be exhausting. You may question, time and time again, what this bleak and scary day is all about? "How on earth am I going to find the strength to go on?" You must trust in your capacity to survive the upheaval if you want to bring joy back to where it belongs.

Take charge of what seems impossible. Give light to those dreams that feel unreachable. Remember – the only way is up! If you believe in life and each day is a blessing despite what you are going through, you will win the day.

A Final Comment

You have come to the end of the book. You have read the beginning, middle and now you have come to the end. I really feel it is important to ask you where you are right now.

Take a moment to reflect upon where you were at the beginning, how you felt during the reading process. Are you at a different place from where you started out?

There may be some parts of this book that completely relate to your current situation whereas other parts spoke in a softer voice, and you didn't quite connect with it in a way you thought you may have.

Being the author of this work I have read through the contents numerous times. Each time I read through a draft I found something different, or understood something from a different angle.

I believe this demonstrates the importance of this type of inspirational book.

Not just to read once, but to read again and again, not only through difficult times, but also the contented moments when you are in the frame of mind to absorb and reflect. The key question for me is, "Do you really want to read this book again?"

Has reading it made you think in a different way about things that are happening or could be about to happen in your life?

I can only vouch for what people have said to me – the feedback I have been offered.

The few chosen people who have read this book state they have had a life changing experience. One person was going through a difficult marriage and she realised that this was not what she wanted anymore, so she decided to start living her life all over again – to live as she wanted to live it and not how others thought she should.

Another was going through a transition where she was feeling quite stuck. After fifteen years in a successful career, she felt she was no longer moving forward. After reading these pages she found herself a new job – a job which would enable her to do the things that had beenmissing during her career charged years.

Yet another person was going through an extremely

sad time after experiencing bereavement after bereavement. She had felt convinced there was no way out of the darkness, but then re-thought and gave herself permission to forgive herself and thus release herself from her own enforced prison.

These are just a handful of the examples.

I am not telling, or even suggesting how you might feel. However, what I am asking of you, is to give yourself the opportunity to feel something and Take Control of your Tomorrow by discovering the real you.

It is dangerous to allow the darkness to cast a shadow over our precious hearts too long. We can't banish the darkness altogether, but we really must allow the light to shine through to balance the quality of our lives.

I really do hope this book has channeled something new into your life – like a shining beacon we all deserve.

Testimonials

"It is a strange thing to admit but this book did change my life!!!"

"This book helped me to look at my life in a way that I realised I was just existing and not living. I had been married at 19, had three children who were now grown up and a husband I did not really know, we lived separate lives, had nothing in common and he was due to retire. Did I want to be with him for another thirty years doing nothing and going nowhere? No! I felt trapped but this book helped me assess my situation."

"This book helped me to construct a list of pros and cons which was frightening as it was so one sided on the cons side. I was frightened to face what I needed to change, but this book gave me the courage to break free and realise that life is for living. I deserved more, I now have the life I want."

"This book asked questions in a way that helped me see what I really wanted and not what everybody else wanted for me. It made me the person I am today happier than I have ever been."

Notes

136

Notes

Printed in Poland
by Amazon Fulfillment
Poland Sp. z o.o., Wrocław

17750015R00083